As soon as Pachelbel Penguin finished talking to Puccini Pooch, he cal... Mozart Mouse. He explained to them how Puccini Pooch was going to be alone at Christmas.

"I have an idea," he continued. "Would all of you like to go with me and surprise him?"

"Of course!" Mozart Mouse agreed. "Come over first thing in the morning, and we will be ready to go."

The City Opera House

The City Opera House is decorated for the Christmas holidays.

1 Clap and count the rhythm pattern on each banner.

2 If the pattern has 4 counts ($\frac{4}{4}$ time), color the sign **red**.

3 If the pattern has 3 counts ($\frac{3}{4}$ time), color the sign **green**.

4 Then color the rest of the picture.

Meanwhile, Puccini Pooch was busy cleaning his apartment, getting ready for Pachelbel Penguin's arrival. He wanted to make sure that everything was neat and tidy. As he worked, he sang his favorite Christmas song.

1. Clap (or tap) *Jolly Old Saint Nicholas* and count aloud evenly.
2. Point to the notes and count aloud evenly.
3. Say the finger numbers aloud while playing them in the air.
4. Play and say the finger numbers.
5. Play and say the note names.
6. Play and sing the words.

MIDDLE C POSITION

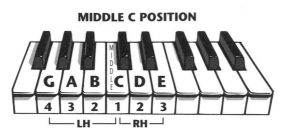

Jolly Old Saint Nicholas

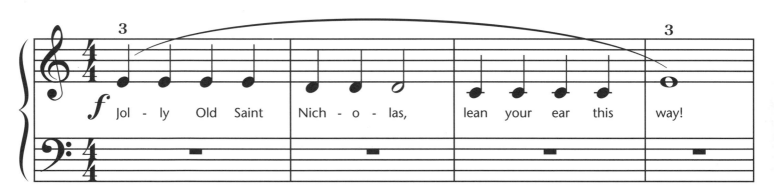

Jol - ly Old Saint | Nich - o - las, | lean your ear this | way!

Student plays one octave higher with duet part.

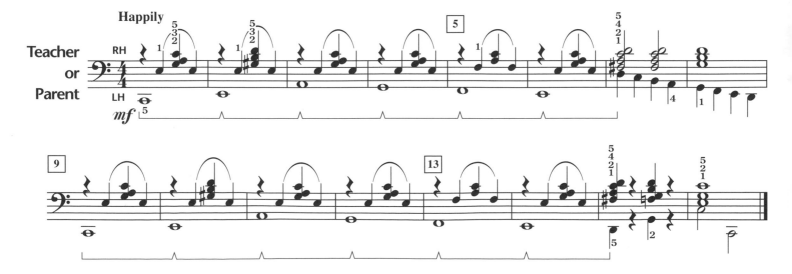

5

Don't you tell a sin - gle soul what I'm going to say;

9

Christ - mas Eve is com - ing soon, now, you dear old man,

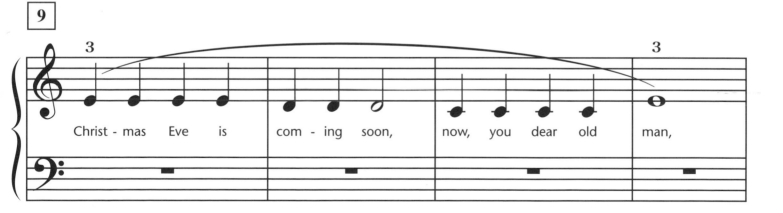

13

Whis - per what you'll bring to me, tell me if you can.

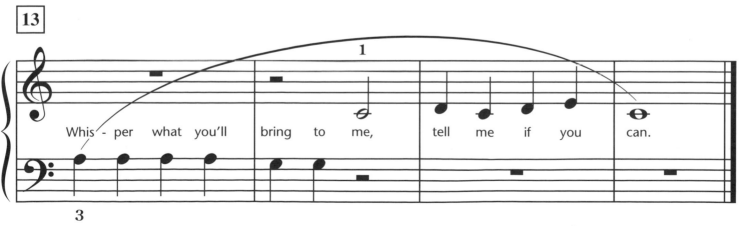

6

The next day was Christmas Eve, and it dawned clear and bright. When the music friends came out of the house to meet Pachelbel Penguin, they were surprised to see a horse and sleigh waiting for them.

"We're going to the city in a one-horse, open sleigh," Pachelbel announced.

"Just like the one in *Jingle Bells*," declared Beethoven Bear.

They quickly loaded the sleigh with their luggage and gifts. As the horse trotted off, everyone began to sing.

1. Clap (or tap) *Jingle Bells* and count aloud evenly.
2. Point to the notes and count aloud evenly.
3. Say the finger numbers aloud while playing them in the air.
4. Play and say the finger numbers.
5. Play and say the note names.
6. Play and sing the words.

Jingle Bells

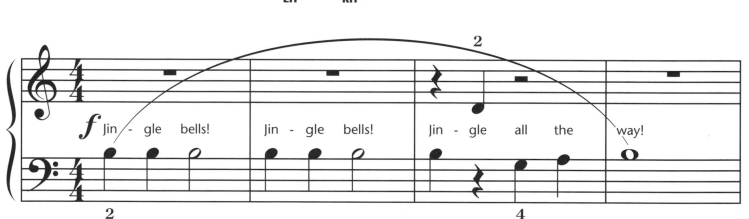

Student plays one octave higher with duet part.

5

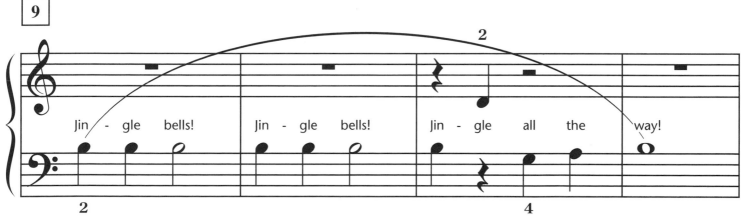

Oh, what fun it is to ride in a one-horse, o-pen sleigh!

9

Jin - gle bells! Jin - gle bells! Jin - gle all the way!

13

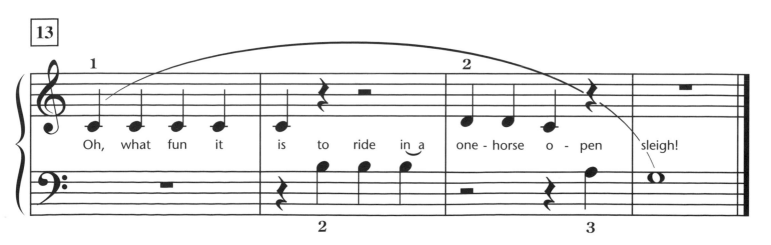

Oh, what fun it is to ride in a one-horse o-pen sleigh!

When they arrived at Puccini Pooch's apartment, Pachelbel Penguin went to the door by himself. Puccini greeted him warmly and they went inside.

A few minutes later, Puccini Pooch heard singing. It sounded like it was in the hall. In fact, it sounded like it was right outside his door!

"It must be Christmas carolers," he said to Puccini Pooch. "They are singing *Up on the Housetop*. Let's see who it is."

1. Clap (or tap) *Up on the Housetop* and count aloud evenly.
2. Point to the notes and count aloud evenly.
3. Say the finger numbers aloud while playing them in the air.
4. Play and say the finger numbers.
5. Play and say the note names.
6. Play and sing the words.

MIDDLE C POSITION

Up on the Housetop

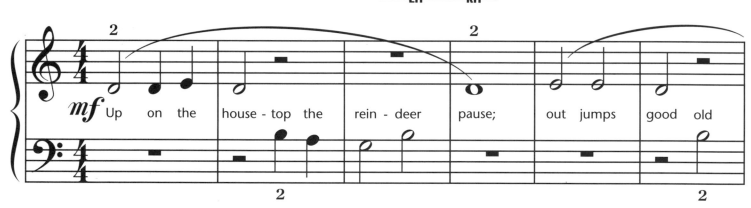

Student plays one octave higher with duet part.

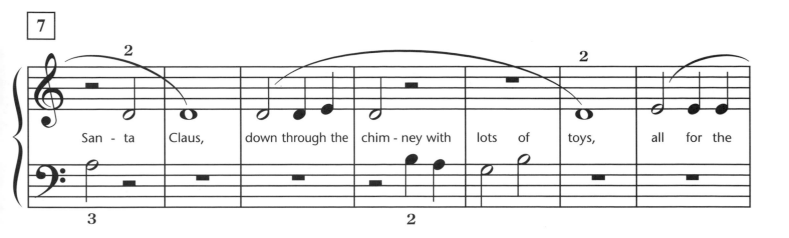

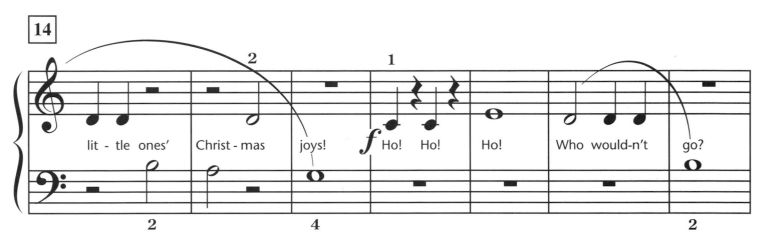

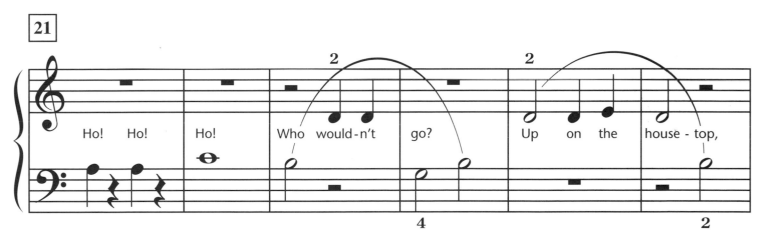

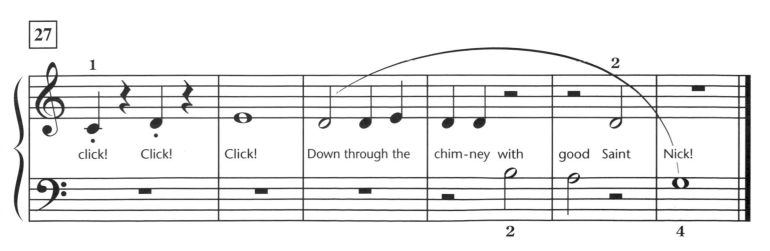

When Puccini Pooch opened the door, he couldn't believe his eyes! There stood Beethoven Bear, Mozart Mouse and all the rest of his music friends, singing a song just for him.

Christmas Caroling

1. Color the area containing an A **red**.
2. Color the area containing a B **pink**.
3. Color the area containing a C **green**.
4. Color the area containing a D **blue**.
5. Color the area containing an E **purple**.
6. Color the area containing an F **yellow**.
7. Color the area containing a G **orange**.
8. Then color the rest of the picture.